Career Exploration

For
Homeschool
High School Students

By
Carol Topp

Ambassador Publishing
Cincinnati, Ohio

Table of Contents

Introduction

You will accomplish a lot as you work though this book! You'll learn a lot about yourself, your personality, careers and jobs, and may be even pick a college to attend! Hopefully, you have a few great ideas to pursue.

As you progress through the book, discuss what you've learned with your parent(s). They can help you chose a college major or make high school education plans to help you be successful in your future life!

If you're taking this as a class with a group, share with each other what you are learning. Compare notes, recommend someone you know that your fellow students can interview or job shadow, ask for their recommendations, and maybe plan to make a college visit together.

I hope you learn more about yourself and a potential future career by the end of this book.

Carol Topp, CPA

Chapter One:
How Can You Know the Rest of Your Life as a Teenager?

Many people see career exploration as trying to pick a career that you will have for your entire life. That's a pretty tall order for a teenager.

Ask any adult if they knew what career they wanted as a teenager and you will find that most adults change careers several times in their life.

Most people see major life decisions such as choosing a career as a target—and they need to hit a bull's-eye—or as a specific path created just for them and they must follow it. If they miss the bull's-eye or stray off the path, they fear they will be miserable because they are living outside some pre-ordained destiny.

Is Life a Bull's-Eye or a Path?

The problem with thinking that life decisions are like archery is that no one tells you how to hit the bull's-eye on the target or how to find the perfect path. Some experts or books try to help, but no one knows the future for themselves, let alone for another person.

Mike was a camp counselor and had lots of teenagers come to his office and ask questions like, "Should I be a doctor or a plumber?"

Mike's answer was, "Be the best doctor or the best plumber you can be." This probably frustrated the teenager asking the question, but Mike was trying to get their thinking off their paths and onto more important things such as their character—to be a person who would be hardworking at whatever career they pursued.

The goal of career exploration is not to pick a career you'll have for the rest of your life. It's to learn a process of discovery and research to make a decision on a career path or college major to pursue. After reading this book, you may not know what you want to be when you grow up, but you will know what direction to take for the next step in your life.

No one knows the future, so don't expect to have your entire adult life figured out as a high school student. All you need to do now is to try and get an idea of what the next phase of your life might hold.

Nobody Knows the Future

Look at Joseph from the Old Testament. If you don't remember who he is, you can look up Joseph's amazing story in the Bible. Look in the Book of Genesis starting in Chapter 37 (skip Chapter 38; it's about Joseph's brother Judah behaving badly). Joseph's story picks up again in Chapter 39 and goes through Chapter 41. Or maybe you've seen the Tim Rice musical, "Joseph and the Amazing Technicolor Dream Coat." It's a pretty accurate telling (except that Pharaoh sounds like Elvis!)

Joseph had several "careers." He worked for his dad tending flocks of sheep and goats and then he was sold into slavery by his jealous brothers. He became a personal attendant, house manager, and financial manager to Potiphar, a big shot in Egypt. Unfortunately, Joseph was falsely accused of attacking Potiphar's wife and landed in prison. While locked up he became a prison supervisor guarding other prisoners, a dream interpreter, and eventually became an advisor to the Pharaoh of Egypt. He organized the storage of food and prevented his family and the entire nation of Egypt from dying of famine.

Joseph could not see how each of these jobs would be used together to accomplish great things in his life, but we can! We know the end of his story.

Unfortunately, you don't know the end of your story yet, but you can do what Joseph did and work hard at every job or career you have. Be the best doctor, plumber, or advisor you can be. You never know how your current job will help in your future.

Not One Career for Life

Many adults change careers and hold several different jobs over their working career. The same will probably be true for you.

I have had these careers in my adult life:
Industrial Engineer
Cost Analyst
Church Treasurer
Nonprofit Consultant
Bookkeeper
Accounting Software Trainer
Certified Public Accountant (CPA)
Author
Public Speaker

See what I mean? I've had lots of careers. I never knew what would be coming next, but I tried to use the skills I was learning in each job for whatever came next. You'll do the same.

When You Will Know What You Need to Know

One of my favorite stories comes from Corrie ten Boom, a Dutch lady made famous for hiding Jews from the Nazis in World War II. Her story is told in the book and movie called "The Hiding Place." Corrie explains that when she was ten years old she asked her father about a term she had read called "sex sin."

"Father, what is sexsin?" He turned to look at me, as he always did when answering a question, but to my surprise he said nothing. At last he stood up, lifted his traveling case from the rack over our heads, and set it on the floor.

"Will you carry it off the train, Corrie?" he said.

"It's too heavy," I said.

"Yes," he said. "And it would be a pretty poor father who would ask his little girl to carry such a load. It's the same way, Corrie, with knowledge. Some knowledge is too heavy for children. When you are older and stronger you can bear it. For now you must trust me to carry it for you."

And I was satisfied. More than satisfied – wonderfully at peace. There were answers to this and all my hard questions. For now I was content to leave them in my father's keeping.

It's a lot like that with us, even though we're not ten years old anymore. For some reason God doesn't tell us everything we want to know about our lives now. We probably couldn't handle it if we did know too much. Like Corrie, who was willing to wait and learn more later, you must be patient. More and more insight and revelations will come as you get older.

Remember me talking about Joseph? He didn't know his life path. It looked pretty dim when his brothers sold him into slavery, but Joseph used every experience to his advantage. It's neat that we get to see his whole story.

So your goal is not to know what you're going to be for the rest of your life! Your goal in career exploration is to try and decide on the next step.

Like a flashlight that only illuminates a few feet in front of you, this book will shed enough light to show you a little bit ahead. Your job is to turn on the flashlight and keep looking.

Additional Reading on God's Will for Your life

If this topic of discerning God's will for your life in interesting to you, read CRU's booklet, *The Art of Discerning God's Will*

You can find at CruPressGreen.com under Sending>Graduating Seniors>Mature Teaching or http://crupressgreen.com/the-art-of-discerning-gods-will/

Jot down notes as you read. It helps retain the information.

What are the ways that you can discern God's will?

Desires and _____

Logic, _____ and a _____ _____

_____

_____

The _____ of Others

_____

Mind, _____, and _____

Chapter Two:
It's Only 4 Steps:
The Career Exploration Process

"At first Andrew didn't want to take your Career Exploration class, but it turned out to be one of his favorites," an enthusiastic mother told me. I had just completed a semester-long class for 8th to 12th graders at my homeschool co-op. The seventeen teenagers relished studying themselves!

Career Exploration Is a Process, Not a Point

The goal of this book is to learn a process. It will teach you the tools that will allow you to search for a future career. My hope is that you will finish this book with three possible careers you could pursue or at least a general idea of a career path to follow.

My own life has had several career explorations. During high school, I decided on a college major: engineering. I considered my skills and abilities, but I didn't consider priorities such as time with family. After I became a mother, my priorities changed and I had another period of career investigation. I found accounting to be to my liking and very flexible. I retrained, became a CPA, and now work as a self-employed accountant. It is an excellent fit of career and family for me.

The 4-Step Career Exploration Process

In order to explore possibilities for the careers you may be interested in, you'll work through these four steps:

1. Investigate: Discover your personality, abilities, skills, and priorities.
2. Match possible careers to your personality.
3. Research potential careers to see if there is a fit.
4. Prepare a plan to pursue your career choice including picking a college.

By way of example, when my daughter Emily was 14, she learned from taking my career exploration class that she was organized, encouraging, and detail oriented.

That's the first step, investigate, which you'll do in Chapter Three.

She took some fun personality tests that matched her traits to several careers (Step 2 which will be covered in Chapter Four Personality Tests). She researched about six of them in detail (Step 3 and Chapters Five through Seven in this book). She rejected some upon learning more about them and ultimately settled on pharmacy, teaching, and accounting.

Emily planned to take biology and chemistry classes in high school. If she liked those subjects, she thought she would pursue pharmacy. If not, she could become an accountant. She also volunteered her time teaching a children's Sunday School class to see if she would enjoy being a teacher. Those were all part of Step 4, her plan, which you will do in Chapter Eight Creating a High School Plan.

See how she went through the four steps? It took her about a month or two to go through the first three steps. The fourth step can take longer. The planning doesn't take too long, but executing the plan can take years, especially for a high school student.

Having a Goal

The last step in the career exploration process is creating an education and experience plan to meet your goals. Think about what classes, part-time jobs, or volunteering you can pursue now to prepare you for the future. If you have a goal in sight, your schoolwork and part-time jobs become more meaningful.

You will learn about graduation requirements in your state and also what most colleges expect in Chapter Eight.

Then you will make a high school plan that is unique to you. In my class, David was a student considering engineering. His plan includes a full load of math and science classes. In contrast, Sarah is interested in acting as a career, so she was encouraged to participate in a summer drama camp run by a local Christian high school.

Life Is an Adventure

The career exploration experience may trigger something dynamic for you. It did in my class. A change occurred as the students began to chart a career path with manageable steps to get there. They became more interested in their classes, started setting goals, and talking about their futures.

I encouraged my students to consider carefully how they spent their time, what kind of classes they selected, and what part-time jobs or volunteer opportunities they pursued. Each decision in life can open doors that will lead you on the path to your goals and dreams. Life is an exciting adventure for teenagers.

I hope you, too, will enjoy investigating your personality, matching it with potential careers, researching occupations to find a good fit, and then executing a plan to reach your goals.

The 4-Step Career Exploration Process:

1. _____-Discover your personality, abilities, skills and priorities.

2. Match possible careers to _____.

3. _____ potential careers to see if there is a fit.

4. _____ to pursue your career choice.

You'll be going through all four of these steps in this book. In the next chapter you'll explore your talents and interests and following that, your unique personality.

Chapter Three:
Who Am I?
Inventory of Your Talents
and Interests

Your Talents and Interests

Naturally, when considering a future career, you should consider your talents and skills. Usually you'll be most successful and happy in a field where you have some natural talent or attained skill. Listing your talents and skills can prompt some career ideas.

Ask your parent(s) and friends for help. They can see talents you have that you don't see. Print off the lists that follow and ask friends and family to check off all the talents and skills that apply to you.

My talents or skills such as playing piano, singing, organization, math, cooking, etc.

Do you need some ideas to kick start your list? Here's list of personal skills. Add all that apply to you to your list of talents.

Baking	Creative-thinking skills
Bilingual	Driving
Building structures	Dusting furniture
Caring for others	Developing plans for projects
Changing a tire on a car	Diplomacy skills
Changing a light bulb	Displaying art
Checking the oil in a car	Distributing products
Cleaning a house or room	Dramatizing ideas
Clearing a drain	Drawing/painting
Changing a diaper	Effective study skills
Coaching a sport	Encouraging people
Communicating with young or old	Enforcing rules
people	Entertaining others
Conflict resolution	Estimating time
Confronting other people	Finding missing information
Constructing buildings	Following instructions
Consulting organizations	First Aid
Counseling people	Following a recipe

Gardening
Gathering evidence
Knowledge of government affairs and politics
Knowledge of current events
Mopping the floor
Mowing the lawn
Organizing a closet, attic, or garage
Organized
Painting a room
Playing a musical instrument
Playing a sport
Promoting events
Proposing ideas
Providing customer service
Providing discipline
Public speaking
Plumbing
Questioning others
Reading a map
Repairing machines
Raking leaves

Risk taking
Running meetings
Selling ideas
Selling products or services
Serving people
Singing
Solving problems well
Taking photographs
Teaching
Thinking logically
Time-management skills
Training skills
Translating words
Tracking personal finances
Tutoring
Vacuuming
Wallpapering
Washing the car
Using computers
Working with statistics
Writing clearly and concisely
Writing letters, papers, or proposals
Mental arithmetic

Here's another list, but it specifically lists skills that employers look for. Add all that apply to your list of skills and talents. Again, hand this list to your parent(s) or friends and get their opinions on which skills you possess.

Making a household budget
Meeting deadlines
Planning
Speaking in public
Supervising others
Accepting responsibility
Instructing others
Solving problems
Managing money or budgets
Managing people
Meeting the public
Negotiating
Organizing or managing projects
Written communications
Dealing with data
Analyze data or facts
Investigate
Keep financial records
Locate answers or information
Calculate, compute
Solving problems
Classify data
Compare, inspect, or record facts
Count, observe, compile
Detail-oriented
Synthesize
Evaluate
Research
Articulate
Inventive
Logical
Ingenious
Write clearly
Design
Develop/Create
Edit
Correspond with others
Remember information
Communicate verbally
Create new ideas
Speak in public
Leadership

Arrange social functions
Motivate people
Competitive
Negotiate agreements
Decisive
Plan
Delegate
Run meetings
Direct others
Self-controlled
Explain things to others
Self-motivated
Get results
Solve problems
Mediate problems
Take risks
Artistic
Music appreciation
Play instruments
Perform, act
Drawing, art
Expressive
Dance, body movement
Present artistic ideas
Using my hands, dealing with things
Assemble or make things
Build, observe, and inspect things
Construct or repair buildings
Operate tools and machinery
Drive or operate vehicles
Good with my hands
Use complex equipment
Endure long hours
Follow directions
File records
Learn quickly
Good attendance
Honest
Arrive on time
Follow instructions
Meet deadlines
Get along with supervisor

Get along with co-workers
Hard-working, productive
Able to coordinate
Friendly
Ambitious
Good natured
Assertive
Helpful
Capable
Humble
Cheerful
Imaginative
Competent
Motivated
Industrious
Conscientious
Thrifty
Creative
Intelligent
Dependable
Intuitive
Discreet
Learn quickly
Eager
Loyal
Efficient
Mature
Energetic
Methodical

Enthusiastic
Modest
Resourceful
Natural
Formal
Open-minded
Optimistic
Sincere
Original
Solve problems
Patient
Spontaneous
Persistent
Steady
Physically strong
Tactful
Practice new skills
Take pride in work
Reliable
Tenacious
Flexible
Responsible
Trustworthy
Self-confident
Versatile
Sense of humor
Well-organized

Your Interests

Now, make a list of your interests. You may have already listed some interests in the previous list, but aim to fill this page with your interests. What do you spend time doing that gives you joy or holds your interest? These may turn into a career, or they may remain a hobby and pleasurable pastime.

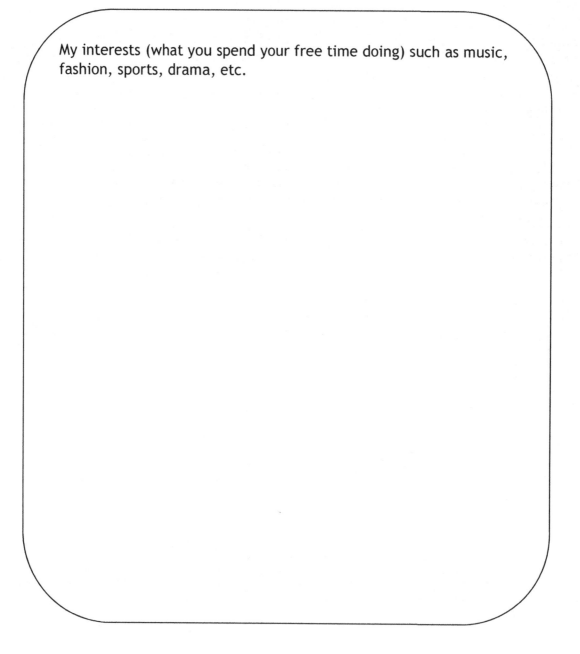

My interests (what you spend your free time doing) such as music, fashion, sports, drama, etc.

Your Values and Priorities

Now it's time to consider your values and priorities in a future job. Following are three lists. Rank each list with numbers from 1 for highest priority and then down in lower priorities.

Again ask for feedback and the opinion of your family, parents, and close friends who know you well. You might be amazed at the insights they have about your values and priorities that you don't see in yourself.

You'll come back to these lists after researching a few careers to see if your choices line up with your priorities.

Life purpose.
What gives your life meaning? Rank these from 1 for highest importance to you to 9 for least important to you.

_____ Serve God

_____ Family

_____ Honesty and Integrity

_____ Friends

_____ Serve Others

_____ Achievement

_____ Make Money

_____ Leisure

_____ Beauty and Art

Work Surroundings
What kind of environment do you want to be in? Rank these from 1 for highest importance to you to 12 for least important to you.

_____ Challenge

_____ Travel

_____ Outdoors

_____ Stability

_____ Organized

_____ Clean Environment

_____ Independence

_____ Equality

_____ Flexible hours

_____ Variety

_____ Adventure and risks

_____ Harmony

Results from work:
What you want from your job or career? Rank these from 1 for highest importance to you to 8 for least important to you.

_____ Recognition

_____ High income

_____ Help others

_____ Intellectual stimulation

_____ Security

_____ Continuing to learn

_____ Leadership

_____ Career progress

Here are two examples of how values and priorities can enter into your career decision.

My dentist knew he wanted to work with people and work with his hands. He worked one summer for his father who was an auto mechanic. He liked the work, but he hated the environment. It was hot, smelly, and greasy. He wanted a clean, quiet environment, so he decided to become a dentist. He still works with his hands and with people, but the environment of his dentist office is clean and quiet.

My brother-in-law decided to become a doctor, but time with his family and time outdoors was important to him. He decided to be a dermatologist (skin doctor), because he could have regular office hours and no on-call emergencies. This allowed him time for his family. He didn't work outdoors, but his high income allowed him to buy a nice camper and take camping trips with his family.

Chapter Four:
You Can't Fail These Tests:
Personality Tests

Personality tests can be a lot of fun to take. There's no studying and no wrong answers! It's also interesting to compare yourself to your friends and family. Have them take some of these tests and compare your answers. You might find you understand your family a lot better!

Before you start these personality tests, let me explain the way they group people. These tests use something they call typology, which is the study of types of people. According to Carl Jung, a Swiss psychologist, all people can be characterized using the following three criteria:

> Extraverts or Introverts

> Sensing or Intuition

> Thinking or Feeling

Dr. Jung did not mean that some people don't think or others don't feel emotions, it just a way he used to describe how we process information and make decisions.

Isabel Briggs Myers created a popular personality inventory and added a fourth criterion: Judging - Perceiving

Let me explain what each of these personality types mean. Each of them represents a continuum between two opposite poles.

Extraversion – Introversion refers to the source of a person's energy. An extravert's source of energy comes mainly from the external world. They get energized by being around people, but an introvert gets energy mainly by being alone.

Sensing – Intuition refers to how someone deals with information. Sensing means that a person believes information that comes directly from the external world. Intuition means that a person believes information that they can interpret and add meaning, usually through personal experience.

Thinking – Feeling has to do with how a person processes information. Thinking means that a person makes a decision mainly through logic. Feeling means that he or she makes a decision based on emotion or based on what they feel they should do.

Judging – Perceiving reflects how a person implements the information he or she has processed. Judging means that a person organizes all of his life events and, as a rule, sticks to his plans. Perceiving means that he or she is inclined to improvise and explore alternative options.

Jung Typology Test

Go to www.humanmetrics.com and take the **Jung Typology Test**. It is free and should take you about 10 minutes.

What are you? _____ (you'll need this later)

Click though some of the links especially the Jung Career Indicator.

Print out or record the list of possible careers. You'll use it later.

What careers did the Jung test recommend?

My tests show I am an ISTJ and some of the careers listed include: Engineering and Accounting. Amazing! Those have been my two major careers.

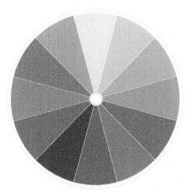

Colorwize Test

Here's a fun, quick test. Use your favorite colors to discover your personality and some careers that might work for you.
http://www.colorwize.com/CareerTestFirst.htm

What color are you?_____

What careers did the Colorwize test recommend?

Keirsey Test

Visit http://www.keirsey.com. This website offers another type of personality test. It classifies people into one of four temperaments.

Click on **"Take the KTS-II!"** in the upper right corner of the website's home page. It asks for an email address, so get your parent(s)' permission first. After you determine your temperament, read about it and good job fits for you.

What is your Keirsey Temperament? _____

What careers did the Keirsey test recommend?

Additional Personality Tests

Here are some more personality tests, but most charge a small fee of $10-$25.

www.careerkey.org—Personality test related to occupations. There is a fee involved of approximately $10, so ask your parent(s)' permission first. *(Parents: This test is well worth the small fee!)*

http://www.truity.com this website lists several personality tests, some free.

www.career.missouri.edu—Click on Career Educator and then Career Assessment. The website offers several career assessments that vary in price from $10 to $30.

Chapter Five:
Career Clusters and
Elimination Round

It's helpful to group careers in to clusters and focus on a cluster where you have talent and interest or where the personality tests you took indicate a strength.

World of Work Map

The World of Work Map found at http://www.act.org/wwm/student.html covers all U.S. jobs. A career area's location on the map is based on its primary work tasks—working with people, data, things or ideas, or a combination.

1. Work with People. You would like a job helping, teaching, counseling, or healing people.

2. Work with People and Data. You like to persuade or influence people to earn money or be leaders in business.

3. Work with Data. You like to work with numbers. You love to organize things.

You are dependable and orderly.

4. Work with Data and Things. You like performing business activities, keeping offices and factories running smoothly.

5. Work with Things. You are technical. You have mechanical or electrical ability. You like tools, computers, instruments, animals, and crops. You like airplanes and transportation.

6. Work with Things and Ideas. You like science and technology and math. You like to investigate things. You like learning.

7. Work with Ideas. You don't like structure. You are creative and expressive. You have imagination and like discussing things.

8. Work with Ideas and People. You like to communicate by writing, speaking, performing, or learning about history or culture.

Which one or two of the eight areas best describe you?

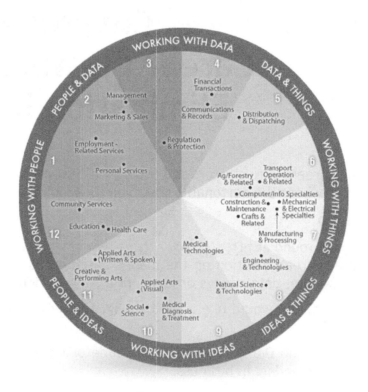

Source: http://www.act.org/world/world.html

If you took the ACT test, you received a personalized report that suggests map regions and career areas on the World of Work Map for you to explore. If you haven't taken the ACT, you can still consider the results of the personality tests from Chapter Four to determine if you prefer to work with people, data, things, ideas, or a combination.

Dig Into the World of Work Map:

Spend some time looking at the interactive version of the World of Work map at http://www.act.org/world/world.html.

1. Start at the outside and work your way in. From your personality surveys, pick one or two areas from the eight listed above that describe you. Find it on the outer rim of the circle.

2. Dig deep. Some of the career groupings don't sound that exciting, so you have to dig deeper. For example no one says, "I really want a career in Distribution and Dispatching," but under that grouping you'll find Air Traffic Controller which is a highly-skilled, well-paid job.

3. Click on some clusters and dig down to specific jobs that sound interesting. Clicking on the job title brings up a window with related occupations. Record the title of jobs that sound interesting. List at least ten, maybe more.

Career Cluster	Job Title

Clicking on the job title pops up a window with data about the job and its salary, availability of jobs, and educational requirements. You'll start doing more research in the coming week. For now, just start compiling a list—a long list.

Eliminate Something

I once asked a teenager if she had any idea of what she wanted for a career. She looked agonized, so I asked if she had any idea of what she *didn't* want to do.

"Oh yeah; I don't want anything to do with science. I hate science," she said.

"OK, good, then there is a huge list of careers you can eliminate. That helps!" I replied.

It's important to eliminate areas that do not fit you (or you as you are right now). It helps you focus on other areas. Very few of us are good at everything!

Can you eliminate any area(s) that you are *not* interested in? List them:

Chapter Six:
Listing and Researching
Possible Careers

Now it's time to move from your personality to possible career choices. You'll start by building a long list of career choices. You're not committed to any career choices yet, so don't omit any possibilities at this point.

1. Use this website to help you match your Myers-Briggs personality indicator from Chapter Four to possible careers:

   http://www.mypersonality.info/personality-types/careers/

2. Go back to the personality tests you took in Chapter Four. Add some possible careers to your list.

3. Look at the career clusters from the World of Work map in Chapter Five and list more careers.

You may not know what some of these career titles mean, but list them anyway. The time for research will come later. Aim for at least 20 possible career choices. If the same career keeps showing on several tests, list it over and over. You're looking for repeats and patterns!

Possible careers to research

Name of Career	Where I heard about it	Why it appeals to me

From your long list of possible careers, did you have any repeats? I hope so. Now you're going to choose three to five careers, especially the ones you saw repeated, and research them more deeply.

List at least three (five is better) career choices that you saw repeated:

_____

_____

_____

_____

_____

Research Careers

There are plenty of places to go for research. We're going to start online and with your local library.

- **World of Work Map** from Chapter Five is a good place to start.

- **Visit the Bureau Labor Statistics website** at stats.bls.gov/oco. Record information about possible careers on the form below including the education required, prospects, and earnings.

- **Professional organizations.** Google the words "careers in your chosen career". Such as "Careers in dentistry" When I did that, I found the American Dental Association (the ADA). On their website you can read about becoming a dentist and watch a video on the dentistry career.

  - **Library.** I know it's old fashioned, but libraries are still a great place to get excellent information. Ask your local librarian to show you books on careers. The section of the library labeled **331.702** will be helpful.

The librarian may also have books in the Reference section (meaning you cannot check them out, but can look at them in the library.

Research **at least 3 careers in depth**. Fill in the charts at the end of this chapter. If you have interest in several careers, fill in more charts with your research again next week or over several weeks.

More Research

You can also do more research on possible careers. All of these sources are helpful:

- **Camps and classes**. Attend a summer camp based on a potential career. Search the internet on "camps for future (your career choice)". You'll find camps for future nurses, lawyers, musicians, etc. Many local colleges sponsor these types of camps. You may even get to live in a college dorm while you attend the camp!

Camp Name	Career Interest	Location	Website

- **Employment or self-employment.** Test a future career by getting a job working in your chosen field.

If a job is hard to find, start a business related to your future career. One teenager, Meghan, wanted to be a professional violinist in high school. She explored this career by starting a micro business offering violin lessons to beginning students. It confirmed her decision to study violin in college.

For more information on starting a micro business visit my website MicroBusinessForTeens.com

Here are some possible careers you can test out by starting a micro business. Add a few more micro businesses related to your career interests.

Career	Micro Business
Teacher	Babysitter/Nanny/Tutor
Artist	Graphic Designer
Accountant	Bookkeeper
Musician	Accompanist, Music Teacher
Writer	Blogger, Editor

- **College course guides**. Look online at several college course guides. Pick a popular college near you or your state university. They will list the type of classes you will take in each major they offer.

For example, I googled "nursing Ohio State University" and it led me to a list of classes nurses take. Ask yourself if studying these classes for four years (or more) would interest you.

My daughter, Sarah, was researching careers in graphic design, photography and video production. When she looked at Taylor University's Media Production major course guide she said, "Mom, I want to take every single one of these classes!" That's when we knew she had hit on a good match. She went on to major in Media Production with an emphasis on Film and a minor in Photography and has loved all her classes in her major.

Career Research

Career		
Description of the work and skills needed (Use keywords)		
Work Environment		
Level of Education		
College classes that sound interesting (from a college course guide)		
Earnings		
Growth Rate/Job Prospects		
Values supported (from Chapter Three)		
Additional Information		

Career		
Description of the work and skills needed (Use keywords)		
Work Environment		
Level of Education		
College classes that sound interesting (from a college course guide)		
Earnings		
Growth Rate/Job Prospects		
Values supported (from Chapter Three)		
Additional Information		

Chapter Seven:
Be in Someone's Shadow:
Interviewing and Shadowing

You've listed your talents and interests, taken personality tests, and done some basic research. Now narrow down your choice of careers to about two or three of your top choices.

Top career choice:_____

Backup choice:_____

Next, you should conduct an interview with someone in your top one or two career fields. The interview can be done over the phone or by email, but in person is much better!

Ask your parent(s), neighbors, and adult friends to help you find a person in your chosen career(s). You could email (or call) a local chapter of a professional organization. Ask for the contact information of someone you can interview. Most adults are very happy to discuss their chosen career and share their experiences with you.

List people you could interview, include their phone number and email address.

Name	Email address	Phone number

Here's a sample email to help you out:

> Dear Mr. Jones,
>
> After taking a career exploration class, I am interested in architecture as a future career. I'd like to arrange a meeting with you to learn more about being an architect.
>
> I'd like to know why you chose to be an architect, its positive and negative aspects, and what training and education is needed. I'm open to any advice you have as well!
>
> Please let me know when you're available. The best days and times for me are: Monday and Tuesday evenings and Saturday afternoons.
>
> If a face-to-face meeting is not possible, may I talk with you over the phone? I won't take more than 15-20 minutes of your time. My phone number is 555-1122.
>
> Thank you for your time. I look forward to talking about architecture with you.
>
> Nick Student

Ask the following questions in your interview. Use the following chart to take notes.

- What are the positive and negative aspects for working in this field?
- Why did you pick this field?
- How do you see jobs in this field changing in the future?
- What type of training or education is required for this work?

- What parts of the job do you find most/least satisfying?
- What personality fits best with this job?

Interview Questions

Name		
Job/Career		
Positive Aspects of career		
Negative aspects of career		
Why did they pick this career?		
Future of this career?		
Training and education required		
Most satisfying part of job?		
Least satisfying part of job?		
Personality that best fits this job		
Additional Advice		

Interview Questions

Name		
Job/Career		
Positive Aspects of career		
Negative aspects of career		
Why did they pick this career?		
Future of this career?		
Training and education required		
Most satisfying part of job?		
Least satisfying part of job?		
Personality that best fits this job		
Additional Advice		

Job Shadowing

Take the interview one step further and ask if you can "shadow" the person for a few hours.

Shadowing means you follow them around as they do their job. Stay quiet and out of the way, but be very observant, take notes, and ask questions if time allows. Job shadowing is very helpful in determining if you would like a career.

True story: Erin thought she wanted to be a forensic scientist (like you see on the television show *CSI*), so she shadowed a coroner. Although the science fascinated Erin, she realized that a forensic scientist spends most of his or her work day alone and in a very quiet environment. It was not at all like the television show! Erin knew she needed to be around people more, so she changed her mind and studied business and marketing in college. The shadowing helped her see the career for what it really is.

Another true story: Emily narrowed her top career choices to accounting and pharmacy. There's not much overlap in those two fields, so she needed to decide on one of them before she went to college. She shadowed two accountants. One accountant operated a small firm with only three employees. Emily observed for about three hours. The other accountant worked for a nonprofit organization. The day Emily visited, two auditors were visiting the nonprofit for their annual audit. It was helpful for Emily to talk to them about why they chose accounting as a college major. They were also pretty close to Emily's age and had lots of advice for her about picking a college major.

Emily also shadowed a pharmacist who had a dream job (for a pharmacist): she worked in a hospital. Emily followed her around for about four hours watching her interact with doctors and patients and spend a lot of time on her computer. It was a true-to-life look at what a pharmacist did all day.

After the shadowing days, Emily took about a month to decide that she liked the working environment of the accountants better than the pharmacist. She was capable of pursuing either career, but seeing the people on the job really helped confirm her decision. She went to college to be an accountant!

Job Shadowing Form

Name		
Job/Career		
Why did they pick this career?		
Future of this career?		
Work environment		
Most satisfying part of job?		
Least satisfying part of job?		
Personality that best fits this job		
Additional Observations		

Chapter Eight:
Creating a High School Plan

Now that you've composed a list of possible careers and done your research, you have a goal to aim for! It's time to create a plan to accomplish that goal. In this chapter you're going to create a high school plan of classes and experiences to be sure you are prepared for your future career.

High School Graduation Requirements

I want you to be prepared for the next phase of your career journey and part of that starts with assessing where you are right now, so let's start with what it takes to graduate from high school.

Since you're homeschooled, start by asking your parent(s) what is required for you to graduate. Your parent(s) and not the State determines graduation requirements for you. That's the freedom of homeschooling, but it's also a huge responsibility. Fortunately, there is some guidance.

State Requirements for Graduation

Start with what your state requires of high school graduates. Google your state and "high school graduation requirements." Hopefully you'll find a list something like this list from Ohio[1]:

> English 4 units (in Ohio a unit is one year, so Ohio students take English all four years of high school))
> Health: ½ unit
> Mathematics: 4 units
> Physical Education: ½ unit
> Science: 3 units
> Social Studies: 3 units
> Electives: 5 units

List your state's requirements on the chart below. Be sure to read the fine print. Ohio had specifics on what type of science classes count for graduation and additional requirements in financial literacy and fine arts.

Subject	State requirement	My parent(s)' requirements	Most colleges' requirements

Your parent(s)' requirement for graduation

I found that state requirements were bare minimum for my daughters, but they served as a good baseline. I thought Ohio's requirement of only 3 years of social studies was not enough and so my daughters took history all four years of high

---

[1] http://education.ohio.gov/getattachment/Topics/What-s-Happening-with-Ohio-s-Graduation-Requiremen/Graduation-Requirements-2014-2017/Graduation-Checklist-2014.pdf.aspx

school in addition to government and economic classes. Additionally, I added a Bible requirement and foreign language requirement.

Ask your parent(s) what they require and add it to the table. They may not have thought through this very much, so give them time and come back to this table later.

True Story: When I taught Career Exploration in my homeschool co-op I assigned this task of researching and listing high school graduation requirements as homework. Heather's mom called me in a panic. She had given no thought to what Heather needed to take in order to graduate. She thought when Heather was old enough, she would be finished with high school, but Heather wanted to be a nurse. That meant some planning in high school to be ready to study nursing in college. Good thing she was taking my class!

What do colleges expect you to take in high school?

As I mentioned earlier, I thought my state requirements were a bare minimum. I wanted my daughters to be ready for college, so I based their high school graduation requirements on what colleges expected to see.

Visit CollegeBoard.com and read the article "High School Classes Colleges Look For" at http://BigFuture.CollegeBoard.org. Click Get In > Your High School Record.

Now fill in the chart again with college requirements and see how things are shaping up.

Your High School Academic Plan

In order to know where you want to go, it's a good idea to figure out where you are starting from. So, next, you're going to create a high school plan. You'll probably need your parent(s)' help with this part, too.

Start by listing what you've already accomplished so far in high school, and then add in what you need to take in your remaining years to be ready for college (or whatever you're planning for next).

High School Plan

Subject	9th grade	10th grade	11th grade	12th grade

Place all required classes in your plan. Choose some electives (that's the fun part!). Review your plan with your parent(s). Make sure you have enough credits to graduate. Make sure you have the right classes to meet your education and career goals.

An example will help. Here's what my daughter's high school plan looked like after her 10th grade year.

Subject	9th Grade	10th Grade	11th Grade	12th Grade
Language Arts	Introduction to Literature	American Literature	*Modern Literature*	*British Literature*
Math	Algebra II	Geometry	*Precalculus*	*Calculus*
Science	Biology	Chemistry	*Physics*	*Adv Chem*
Social Studies	Ancient History	US History	*Modern History*	*Government and Economics*
Foreign Language	Spanish 2	Spanish 3	*Spanish 4*	*Spanish CLEP Prep*
Arts	Art Appreciation	Piano	*Piano*	*Piano*
Health/Phys Ed	Health	Phys Ed	*Phys Ed*	
Electives	Personal Finance and Career Exploration	SAT Prep	*Accounting*	*College Search*

The last two years are in italics because they are what we planned. As it turned out, there were some changes to this plan. Emily never took advanced chemistry. By the time she reached her senior year, she had decided to study accounting in college and didn't need advanced chemistry. See how planning can help?

In reality, my actual plan had more details like where she might take a class (such as our local co-op or a tutor) and what curriculum she might use. But for your use, you don't need those details here.

True Story: From taking my Career Exploration class, Megan had decided she wanted to study violin performance in college and be a professional musician. Her mother wanted her to take physics in her senior year and I was trying to save poor Megan from that fate! She was not good at science and she didn't need another science class to get into music school. I was able to persuade her mother to drop physics and Megan was very grateful.

Match High School Plan to College Requirements

You've come a long way in your planning. Now you'll see how your current high school plan matches with your career goals.

Compare your high school plan to the research you did in Chapter Seven. What you're looking for here is what you need to study in high school to be ready for college. For example, engineering majors need to study math through calculus in high school. If you don't study calculus, you'll be behind the other engineering students in your freshman year. College is hard enough, you don't want to start out behind.

True Story: Jordan decided in his sophomore year that he wanted to be an engineer. Unfortunately, he had not started college-prep math classes early enough, so in his sophomore year he took *both* geometry and algebra II. I usually saw Jordan looking pretty tired that year, but he persevered and is now finishing his engineering degree in college.

You probably don't know what college you want to attend yet (Chapter Nine will help with that), so just chose a few local colleges, your state university, and a few "stretch" schools—colleges you consider a bit beyond your academic reach. Research what their admission requirements are for your particular major or career.

Local college	
Another local college	
State university	
Another state university	
"Stretch" school	
Another stretch school	

For example, here's what MIT recommends of its applicants[2]:

- One year of high school physics
- One year of high school chemistry
- One year of high school biology
- Math through calculus
- Two years of a foreign language
- Four years of English
- Two years of history and/or social sciences

My alma mater, Purdue University, lists what specific high school classes it

---

[2] http://mitadmissions.org/apply/prepare/highschool

expects from applicants. The science, pharmacy, and nursing majors have tougher requirements. Purdue also recommends AP (Advanced Placement) classes.[3]

College Entrance Requirements

College Major:_____

College Name		
English		
Math		
Science		
Social Studies		
Foreign Language		
Other		

Do this again for an alternative college major. It's always a good idea to have a backup plan.

College Major:_____

College Name		
English		
Math		
Science		
Social Studies		
Foreign Language		
Other		

---

[3] http://www.admissions.purdue.edu/apply/highschoolcourses.php

Now go back to your high school plan and see if you're on track to meet the college entrance requirements for your major. Discuss this with your parent(s). Change your plan if needed.

True Story: Brittany wanted to be a professional singer. Her mother encouraged this and paid for voice lessons. In her senior year Brittany changed her mind and chose to become a nurse instead. Unfortunately, she had not prepared herself by taking enough science classes in high school, so during her senior year, Brittany doubled up on biology and chemistry. I wish she had thought through her career options a little earlier in high school and had created a backup plan.

Beyond The Books

High school is more than classes and book learning. There's a wealth of experiences you should take advantage of that can also help you choose a future career.

It's time to create an experience plan. Jot down some experiences that you want to pursue that will help you test out a career. Consider camps, clubs, hobbies, volunteering, jobs or starting a business, books or self-teaching.

Experience Plan

Possible Career			
Job or micro business			
Volunteering			
Camps			
Clubs			
Hobby			

Chapter Nine:
Preparing for College

Your career choice might involve going to college. It's a big task to pick a college and there are many books, websites, and services to help you get started. This chapter is not as comprehensive as a full book or website, but it will point you to some great resources and offer tips and advice.

College Fairs

Visit a college fair in your sophomore or junior year of high school. The biggest college fairs are listed at the National Association for College Admission Counseling website, www.nacacnet.org, and the North American Coalition for Christian Admissions Professionals website, www.naccap.org.

There are also specialized groups that have fairs. Exploring College Options Consortium represents Ivy League schools (www.exploringcollegeoptions.org), Colleges That Change Lives (www.ctcl.org), Historically Black Colleges and Universities (www.hbcufair.com), and Performing and Visual Arts fairs (www.nacacnet.org/college-fairs/PVA-College-Fairs).

When you go, gather up lots of brochures. Ask the college representatives if they have the major you're interested in. Ask if they any local alumni you can contact for shadowing or interviewing.

College fairs in my area	Date	Location	Specialty

Research Online

CollegeBoard.org

CollegeBoard.org is a huge website. It allows you to compare college size in terms of the number of students (including the guy-girl ratio), incoming SAT/ACT scores, distance from home, cost of tuition and other expenses, student makeup (what states they come from, racial makeup of the students, men-women ratio).

I recommend you create an account or download the app and start creating some comparisons of colleges. Also spend a little time reading the articles and watching the videos about college. CollegeBoard.org also has some great planning tools and calendars so you don't miss important application deadlines.

Reviews by Students

There are also several college review websites, usually with forums by students, alumni, or parents. These frequently have negative comments about the colleges. Take these negative remarks with a huge grain of salt. Understand that everyone thinks college cafeteria food is bad, the professors are too hard, and that the girls on campus are not pretty enough!

Here's a list of 25 sites of college reviews by students:
http://onlineuniversityrankings2010.com/2010/top-25-sites-for-real-college-reviews-by-students/ or just search for "Top 25 sites college reviews."

Admission Requirements

Every college has different application requirements, but most focus on SAT/ACT scores and your high school transcript. Some want their application filled out, other colleges will take the Common Application which you can find here: https://www.commonapp.org

Since you a homeschooled student, you will find this article, "Each College is Unique" by Lee Binz very helpful: http://www.thehomescholar.com/each-college-is-unique.php

What are some of the things Lee warns you about when reading admission guidelines?

In Chapter Nine you created a high school plan and compared it with what your career goals are. Now that you've looked at college admission requirements. It's time to update that chart.

College Visits

After you have done some research on colleges, it's time to pack up your mom and/or dad and pay these colleges a visit. Fall or spring is the best time to visit because students will be on campus. Summer may be convenient for you, but the campus has a different look and feel when the students are not there.

I think a college visit-including staying overnight in the dorm-is crucial. Yes, it's expensive and time consuming to travel and pay for a hotel for your parent(s) (you stay in the dorm), but college is a huge investment and you don't want to mess it up.

Here are two great articles on making college visits by Lee Binz:

"Visit Colleges in the Spring" at http://www.thehomescholar.com/Recent-Articles/visit-colleges-in-the-spring.php or simply search for "Lee Binz Visit College Spring."

"Three Steps to Finding a College" (Search for "Lee Binz 3 Steps Find College") http://www.thehomescholar.com/three-steps-to-finding-a-college.php

List some things Lee recommends you do and look for on a college visit:

I've recorded a podcast on the topic of choosing a college. Listen to it at http://DollarsandSenseShow.com and look for Episode #22 Picking a College."

Another great podcast called "Making College Visits Count" by my friends Hal and Melanie Young can be found here: http://ultimateradioshow.com/mbflp-making-college-visits-count

Record some of the tips you gather from the podcasts here:

True Story: We visited a college in a northern state with my daughter Emily. She had done her research online and thought this college might be a good fit for her. We even knew a few students who attended there. The tour of the campus was good and the admission people were helpful. We picked her up after staying overnight in the dorm, and she said, "I'm glad we came to visit, but I am *not* going to this college!" "What happened? Were the girls in the dorm unkind?" we asked. Emily explained that the girls were friendly, but the topics they had to study and write papers about were disgusting to her. Only from staying in the dorm did she pick up on the very liberal leaning of this college, which was not to Emily's liking. Their liberal bent was not apparent from their brochures or the admissions counselor.

We also visited another college that again looked great after researching. When we picked her up from the dorm Emily said, "I can see myself here." That was key. She eventually applied, was accepted, and went to this college (Grove City College in Pennsylvania).

Read College Material

Colleges love to create glossy brochures, but you need to read beyond that. Read several editions of the official student newspaper and the "underground" or unofficial newspaper if you can find one. These will give you an idea of what activities are happening on campus and what issues are debated on the op-ed page.

Pick up a copy of the class course guide (or view it online). This is a listing of what classes you will take in your chosen major. Can you see yourself interested in these classes?

Compare the classes listed between colleges. You may get an understanding of the academic quality of each college. Ask someone from your chosen career to help you compare classes listed in the course guide. Since I'm an accountant, I can tell you which colleges have a stronger academic program in accounting by looking at the course guide.

True Story: My daughter Sarah had been doing research on colleges knowing she wanted to study visual media production and photography. This is a new major and colleges call it by different titles, so it was really important to compare colleges by looking at the classes they offered. I showed her the classes for Media Production at Taylor University and she said, "Mom, I want to take *every one* of these classes!" A visit to the campus and an overnight stay in the dorm confirmed her decision to go to Taylor.

Finally, read a copy of the rules of the college. It may take a bit of digging online to find these rules or ask your tour guide and admissions counselor. On one college visit a parent asked about curfews and dress codes. The student tour guide was reluctant to admit that there was a curfew and a dress code. It was not mentioned anywhere in the campus literature given to us. A student at a Christian college complained about all the rules including mandatory chapel attendance five times a week. Apparently he didn't know about this when he decided to go to college there!

After the College Visit

In Chapter Eight you created a high school plan and compared it with what your career goals are. Now that you've visited a few colleges and learned what they expect to see in high school applicants, it's time to update that chart. Will you be ready to succeed in college? Discuss this with your parents and alter your plan if needed.

Conclusion

Well, you made to the end of the book. If you read it all and did everything I recommended, you have accomplished a lot. You've worked through a process that not many high school students go through.

I hope you have a better understanding of yourself and a few good ideas of a career to pursue.

Don't be afraid if you're still a bit undecided. You can go through this process (or parts of it) again and again. You now have the tools to conduct another career search when in college or later in your life.

Feel free to share what you learned with me. You can email me at Carol@CarolToppCPA.com

I also appreciate your reviews of this book on Amazon.com or other online booksellers.

Carol Topp, CPA

About the Author

Carol Topp, CPA, has had three major careers in her life: engineer, accountant and now author. She has written several books including the *Micro Business for Teens* series, *Homeschool Co-ops: How to Start Them, Run Them and Not Burn Out*, *Business Taxes and Tips for Writers*, and *Teens and Taxes: A Guide for Parents and Teenagers*.

Carol's publications include numerous articles, podcasts, and webinars about money management, micro business, entrepreneurship, and homeschooling. Her articles have appeared in *The Old Schoolhouse*, *Molly Green*, *Home Education*, and *Home School Enrichment* magazines. In addition, Carol has enjoyed conducting workshops at homeschool conventions across the country.

Carol's podcast, *The Dollars and Sense Show*, is part of the Ultimate Homeschool Radio Network. She also hosted the public television program, *Starting a Micro Business* and won a Best Accounting blog award in 2014.

She and her husband live in West Chester, Ohio. They have two grown daughters, both who were homeschooled through high school and are now looking forward to their first careers.

Carol can be contacted through her website CarolToppCPA.com, all over social media, and on Twitter at @CarolTopp.

Offer your feedback, please!

I'd like your honest input on this book and how to improve it.

Please answer the following questions and give them to your instructor or give your feedback online at: http://CarolToppCPA.com/CareerFeedback

How was the amount of homework?
- ❏ Too much
- ❏ OK
- ❏ Pretty easy

Did you end up with 2 or 3 realistic career possibilities?
- ❏ No
- ❏ Maybe
- ❏ Yes

Comments: _____

Do you have a pretty solid plan for high school?
- ❏ No
- ❏ Somewhat
- ❏ Yes, pretty clear

Comments: _____

What was the worst homework assignment?
- ❏ Personality tests
- ❏ Researching careers
- ❏ Calling someone to interview
- ❏ High School Plan
- ❏ Researching colleges
- ❏ Other:_____

What was the most beneficial homework assignment?
- ❏ Personality tests
- ❏ Researching careers
- ❏ Calling someone to interview
- ❏ High School Plan
- ❏ Researching colleges
- ❏ Other:_____

Please give me any additional comments about the book. I appreciate your honesty!

Made in the USA
Las Vegas, NV
15 December 2022

62627180R00039